DIESEL LOCOMOTIVES ON SCOTTISH RAILWAYS

Colin J. Howat

AMBERLEY

First published 2018

Amberley Publishing
The Hill, Stroud
Gloucestershire, GL5 4EP

www.amberley-books.com

Copyright © Colin J. Howat, 2018

The right of Colin J. Howat to be identified as
the Author of this work has been asserted in
accordance with the Copyright, Designs and
Patents Act 1988.

ISBN 978 1 4456 7622 7 (print)
ISBN 978 1 4456 7623 4 (ebook)

British Library Cataloguing in Publication Data.
A catalogue record for this book is available from
the British Library.

Origination by Amberley Publishing.
Printed in the UK.

Introduction

Diesel locomotives on Scottish railways include locomotives from the humble Class 08 shunter right up to the most powerful Class 70 General Electric locomotive, and many others in between. Starting with the Class 08s, or the most common shunting locomotive, these locos are fast becoming a rarity on our current rail system, with the larger main line locos performing the job of marshalling trains. With its basic design coming from the pre-war locomotives operated by the Big Four railway companies, the BR standard diesel shunting loco was a direct follow on of the final LMS design. Using 350 hp, this shunter went on to prove to be a very reliable, strong and simple loco to operate. Over 1,000 of these locos were built, and examples could be found in all corners of Scotland. Originally they were painted in black, then green, and later into BR blue. Since the 1990s, with rail privatisation, many other liveries have appeared.

By far the most successful of the early diesels was the English Electric Class 20. They were ordered under the Modernisation Plan of the 1950s and were initially known as the Type 1s. They had a single cab and later became re-classified as Class 20. These locos were built at both the Vulcan Foundry at Newton-le-Willows, Merseyside, and at the Robert Stephenson & Hawthorns Ltd factory at Darlington. Some of the fleet became very reliable and were well liked by train crews, and their versatility allowed them to operate in pairs or on their own. Their durability saw them outlast all other small Type 1 locos and they can still be found on the UK network. A small batch of Class 20s were taken over by Hunslet Barclay, based in Kilmarnock, in 1988 for weed control train operation and were some of the first private locos to be authorised over BR tracks. Under privatisation, the fleet saw a new lease of life, with over twenty being bought by Direct Rail Services in 1999. Many others were also taken over by various private operators. A small number also saw use in the building of the Channel Tunnel.

The Type 2s, later re-classified as Class 24 and 25 locos, were designed by BR as a replacement for low-powered steam traction. The standard Type 2 fleet eventually ran to 478 locomotives. They were built over a ten-year period, starting in 1958. To speed up production, Class 24 and 25 locomotives were constructed at BR Derby, Crewe and Darlington. A small batch were also constructed by Beyer Peacock in Manchester. The standard Type 2s were a true universal design and operated throughout the UK from the Southern Region in Kent to the north of Scotland. Some of the Class 25 locos were later converted to electric train heating locos (ETHEL) in the mid-1980s when there was a shortage of ETS-fitted Class 37s for the West Highland Line. Class 21 locos, later re-classified as Class 29 locomotives, were built at the North British Works at Springburn in Glasgow, but were initially not successful. Nineteen of the batch were later re-engined at Glasgow Works but, despite more powerful engines, started to be withdrawn from 1969.

Class 26 and 27 locos were built by the Birmingham Carriage & Wagon Works. These locos were originally delivered to the Eastern Region, where they took over suburban and outer suburban services. Other Class 26s and 27s were delivered new to Scotland, while other batches were delivered to the London Midland Region. After a few months in service, the British Rail Board (BRB) decided to transfer all these locos to depots in Scotland. With the modernisation of the important Edinburgh to Glasgow Queen Street line taking place from May 1971, high-speed running of this route was trialled in the late 1960s with Class 27s and later 37s. The BRB eventually agreed to deploy pairs of modified Class 27s operating top and tail with rakes of modified Mk 2 coaching stock to replace the ageing Class 126 DMUs. The locos were fitted with electric train supply (ETS). Sadly, the hammering received on this route led to some unreliable performances, but in time they settled down and worked well until they were replaced in October 1979 by the more powerful Class 47s and Mk 3 coaching stock. Both the Class 26s and 27s remained in front line service until 1993 and 1987 respectively. Fortunately, a sizable number have been preserved all over the UK.

The Class 33s were built by the Birmingham Carriage & Wagon Company and were the one of the most popular diesel locos of all time. They were based in England, and I mention them simply as some ventured into Scotland on various specials in the twilight of their careers. The same applies to the Class 58 locos; again based in England, a few ventured into Scotland on the odd special.

The popular English Electric Class 37s were introduced from 1960 and went on to total over 300 in all. Nobody would have thought back then that they would still be in service over fifty years later. It quickly emerged that a more powerful locomotive than the Type 2s was required. Orders were placed with English Electric for Type 3 power, which later became the Class 37. However, crews did not like the design, and after just over 100 locos were built, there was a change in construction policy. This resulted in the centre nose doors being removed. Class 37s fitted with nose end doors had headcode boxes put on either side of the connecting central doors. Later locos also had roof horns that were mounted centrally between the middle cab windows. When introduced, the maximum service speed was 90 mph, although some specified locomotives were temporarily authorised at higher speeds as part of acceleration trials. Following later refurbishment, most had their maximum speed reduced to 80 mph. By March 1963 most of the Class 37s had been built. In 1967 the Western Region of BR decided that the Hymek diesel locos were to be used on Welsh coal traffic flows and this resulted in a huge re-allocation of the 37s based there. Some were also sent to Scotland for the first time. Members of the class were allocated to Polmadie, Eastfield and Haymarket depots. Some that had been transferred to Scotland were considered for push-pull working between Glasgow Queen Street and Edinburgh. During the 1970s, the Class 37s settled down to become the backbone power of Scotland. Major refurbishments and life extensions continued in the 1980s, and many can still be found on passenger and freight work.

Class 44–46 diesels or Peaks were introduced again in the early 1960s. Ten Class 44 locos were allocated to Derby but were soon transferred to Camden in London. When the production locos (later Class 45) emerged from Derby and Crewe Works, the majority were allocated to Derby, Cricklewood and Toton. The Class 46s were similar to their sister Class 45s with a few modifications. The Peak family remained largely on the Midland Main Line until they were displaced by the new high-speed trains (HST) from 1982. Most of them visited Scotland via the Waverley and G&SW routes. However, they were eventually banned from Glasgow Central from 1981 after a number of derailments in the jungle area outside the station.

Class 50s were introduced from 1968. They were the first main line diesels to be delivered in all-over rail blue. Originally owned by English Electric and leased to BR, the fleet was soon purchased by BR, and after completion of the WCML to Glasgow Central in 1974, were transferred to the Western Region. Most of the Class 50s ventured all over the south-west of Scotland and were regularly seen between Dumfries and Kilmarnock, and even as far south as Girvan and as far north as Inverness. These locos had slow speed control fitted but as the class were very rarely employed on freight work this was hardly ever used. They were fitted for multiple operation and a total of fifty were made. After being transferred to the Western Region in 1972, not many ever ventured back to Scotland again, apart from a few that came up on specials. However, most sadly returned to be scrapped at MC Processors at Springburn in Glasgow.

Possibly the ultimate in the early diesels were the Class 55s, or the Deltics. They were introduced from May 1961 on the East Coast Main Line (ECML) and also worked north of Edinburgh to and from Aberdeen. Occasional workings resulted in visits to the Central Scotland area. From 1978, however, HSTs began to take over from them on expresses from Edinburgh to London King's Cross, and the Deltics began to spread their wings to other parts of Scotland. On several occasions during the summer of 1979, they were even diverted over the Glasgow & South Western Line via Dumfries and Kilmarnock due to various problems on the ECML and WCML. Throughout their careers, the 55s had very few modifications apart from the fitting of electric train heating (ETS). In 1968 the BRB decided that the future in high-speed rail was in unit formations, so even the great Deltics' lives had already been decided.

The Class 56 locos were introduced from 1976 as there was a new requirement for a dedicated freight locomotive due to various external factors including the price of fuel made worse by the then Middle East crisis, which pushed up the price of oil. The BRB were instructed by the government to get more coal transported between the mines and the power stations and this resulted in the creation of the Class 56 loco. The original sixty locomotives were provided by Electroputere of Craiova in Romania, and the rest of the fleet was built by BREL at Crewe. Many of these locos survived well into the privatisation era although by April 2004 the last official workings in the UK took place. Since then a number of the locos have been taken on by Colas and various other private operators, and some have been exported.

Following sectorisation of BR in the late 1980s, it was soon identified that a heavy freight locomotive was needed. An order was placed with Brush Traction of Loughborough for 100 Class 60 locos. Most of this Class have been seen in Scotland, particularly on the once busy Ayrshire coal workings. Once constructed, the Class 60s were allocated to the four Trainload Freight businesses – coal, construction, metals and petroleum. Allocations were spread between Stewarts Lane, Immingham, Thornaby, Toton and Cardiff. Many were given smaller exams and maintenance at Ayr depot. When privatisation finally came in 1996, the four Trainload Freight businesses were sold to North & South Railways, the UK operating arm of the US-based Wisconsin Central Railroad. This company was soon renamed English, Welsh & Scottish Railways (EWS). They stated at the time that all Class 60s would be retained; however, within a short space of time after the General Motors Class 66 locos started to arrive, the Class 60s began to be stored. The decline continued until 2009 and as few as fifteen locos remained in traffic. Since 2012, many have been refurbished, but many others still lie in storage as unserviceable, mainly at Toton.

The success of the Class 59 in the mid-1990s on aggregate trains made EWS decide in around 1995 to start importing Class 66s, which were built in Ontario, Canada. Deliveries of the Class 66 started in early 1998, with batches usually of twelve being delivered to the port of Immingham, west of Grimsby. The new locos were built with standard pneumatic buffers, a central coupling hook and shackle.

From loco No. 66201, swing-head semi-auto couplers were installed from new, with all pre-delivered locos being retrofitted. Deployment in the UK was rapid with the entire EWS network quickly seeing Class 66 activity. By early 1999 Freightliner showed their interest in the Class 66 design and further orders were placed. The first Freightliner locos, Nos 66501 and 66502, were delivered to the UK in July 1999. Due to winning an infrastructure contract from Railtrack, Freightliner ordered a further eighteen Class 66 locos. From 2002 other operators such as GBRf and DRS also ordered these locos, and by the end of 2003 Freightliner continued to add more to its fleet, reaching fifty locos. By the summer of 2004, GBRf placed another order and the success story continued with further deliveries. GBRf also bought Euro Class 66s; however, one of the problems in bringing in these locos was the wrap-round driver's desk. Love them or hate them, the Class 66 looks to be the dominant freight loco for the foreseeable future.

The Class 67 fleet emerged as a direct result of the UK rail privatisation process as well and they were ordered by EWS. It was quickly agreed that the new motive power was required to operate in the UK freight sector mainly on high-speed trains. EWS again turned to General Motors. They stipulated that they needed a loco capable of 125 mph with electric train heating (ETS) based on a four-axle bogie. General Motors were agreeable and a partnership was formed with Alstom. EWS ordered thirty Class 67s, which were assembled at the Alstom plant in Valencia, Spain. All were delivered by 2000. The locos were immediately deployed on Royal Mail contract services to and from Scotland and elsewhere, but sadly in 2004 this work was lost as road and air competition priced EWS out of the market. A limited mail operation is still operated from Shieldmuir Depot, south of Motherwell, using Class 325 electric units. In subsequent years, the fleet has found many new walks of life. From 2004 the Class 67s took over the diesel legs of the ScotRail Sleeper services to Inverness and Aberdeen, and the Fort William legs from 2006. Further passenger work came from ScotRail on the Fife Circle services due to shortages of DMUs. Apart from Class 43 HST power cars, these are the only diesel locos capable of 125 mph.

HSTs, or Class 43 locos, were designed as a short-term answer for the new long-distance modern trains required to compete with the growing motorway network and short-haul air travel. The introduction of the prototype train was a protracted affair following major trade union issues relating to manning locos at high speeds, with ASLEF demanding two drivers on trains travelling at over 100 mph. The BRB's wish for over 150 seven- or eight-car HST sets was rejected by the government of the time and eventually just ninety-five sets were built. However, with time these sets demonstrated that they were well suited to the internal UK high-speed market and went on to be the backbone of inter-city travel. Originally, the Class 43 HSTs were launched for use in the Western, Eastern and Scottish regions. The Midland Main Line route also benefited from them as well.

By the mid-1960s most developed countries in the world were upgrading their rail infrastructure and trains. On privatisation of the UK network in the mid-1990s, the HST fleet became the property of the Angel and Porterbrook Leasing businesses. However, huge changes were in the air and many Class 43s transferred to many other parts of the UK network. Some benefits came from the InterCity marketing campaign combined with service improvements but the lack of government conviction about rail travel and the almost total lack of real investment slowed down what few plans were on the table. The government of the day put a stop to many plans to develop a UK version of the Japanese high-speed network linking the most important and heavily populated locations. It was soon realised by the BRB that with no government support for an improved railway in the UK, an effort had to be made to try and raise speeds on the existing rail network without compromising safety. Major track works took place at a number of locations throughout Scotland, with restrictive curves being ironed out, which allowed train speed increases, while canting of the track was adopted in other situations, which also increased speeds. Mk 2 coaching stock then emerging from the BREL Derby Works was upgraded to operate at 100 mph. Assembly of the two prototype power cars, Nos 41001 and 41002, was undertaken at BREL Crewe Works, and then they were transferred to Derby for completion. The cab design was new to the UK and not welcomed by the trade unions. A soundproof door gave access into the engine compartment and the cab and engine bays were separate modules with sound insulation between them in an attempt to provide an improved working environment for the driver. At an early stage in the design it was agreed that the HST formations would comprise seven or eight coaches with power cars at either end to provide the maximum speed of 125 mph.

The problem with selecting such a single high-output engine and alternator was weight. It was stipulated that a minimum vertical dynamic force between wheel and rail was very important to gain certification for 125 mph running over existing tracks. As a result axle load and unsprung mass on each power car had to be kept to a minimum. With no single diesel available to give the required 4,500 hp, it was agreed that two power cars, one at each end of a formation with a reduced 2,250 hp, would be the way forward. Developments of through train control made it possible for both engines to be used for traction and auxiliary power at the same time. Paxman, based at Colchester, were able to offer a suitable twelve-cylinder engine. The driving cabs were made of glass fibre reinforced with plastic constructed to 50 mm thickness, affording train crews the best possible protection at maximum speed. The body structure for the associated coaches was formed of a steel frame with a welded stressed steel skin. To maintain the smooth and streamlined aesthetic appearance of the train, all underside equipment between the bogies was mounted in easy to remove modules with either hinged or detachable exterior doors.

The passenger environment was important in the design of the HST, and this led to the use of double glazing, full air conditioning and improved interior sound insulation. A high-quality public address system was also incorporated. In terms of seating, the design was similar to that used in the Mk 2 vehicles. The initial plan was to operate each train set with two buffet vehicles. The catering equipment was housed on the two seat side of the buffet car and there was a staff compartment with lockers. Ovens and fridges were located on the bulkhead adjacent to the staff area. Adjacent to the kitchen were the cooking and preparation areas with a bar facing the corridor side of the coach.

By early 1973, all the prototype HST vehicles had been delivered from Litchurch Lane, Derby. Later in the year, on 2 August, a special was run from London King's Cross to Darlington, which conveyed the Rt Hon. Richard Marsh, Chairman of the then BRB. Various MPs and press from all over the world also travelled on the special. The train was put through its paces and hit 125 mph south of York.

The Scottish Region took delivery of the first production trains from May 1978. By the summer of 1985, power car prototype No. 43000 was handed over to the National Railway Museum at York, where it was cosmetically restored to full working order. Prior to the introduction of the production HSTs to the Western Region, another major hurdle had to be overcome – that of driver training. This took approximately three weeks per driver. A further twenty-seven HST sets were introduced to the Eastern Region from the beginning of 1978, with certain sets being allocated to Craigentinny, Edinburgh. The first set for Heaton Depot, Newcastle, arrived in August 1977. It had been planned to upgrade the power on these units, but technical issues compounded by the desire to maintain a common fleet saw the upgrade cancelled.

The success of the HST fleet continued, and by the late 1970s the BRB submitted further requests to the government for more sets due to severe overcrowding, particularly in the

Eastern Region. Authority was granted but the order was eventually reduced. By 1980 there was a decrease in passengers travelling, which allowed easier diagramming of sets, particularly on the Western Region. HSTs were finally transferred to the Midland Main Line from the end of 1982, and in the same year HSTs were diagrammed to and from Inverness and Aberdeen. Others have been diagrammed in Scotland between Glasgow Queen Street and London King's Cross via Edinburgh; others have been diagrammed over the WCML for cross-country services and other units have even worked over the G&SW between Kilmarnock and Dumfries on booked and diverted cross-country services.

Following the electrification of the ECML in 1989, most HST sets were re-allocated around the UK, but many still operate in Scotland today. Most are used between Inverness and Aberdeen to London King's Cross. Most were replaced by Class 221/222 Voyagers from 2005. However, the Class 43s are arguably the most successful diesel locomotives ever made in the UK. Some of the diesel traction mentioned in this book can still be experienced at various preservation groups throughout Scotland.

DEPOT CODES

AY – Ayr
BR – Bristol Bath Road
CD – Crewe Diesel
CL – Colas Rugby
DT – Dunfermline Townhill
DR – DRS Carlisle
ED – Eastfield Glasgow
FL – Freightliner Leeds
FP – Finsbury Park London
GB – GB Railfreight Doncaster
GD – Gateshead
HA – Haymarket
HM – Healey Mills
HT – Heaton
HQ – Headquarters (BR)
IM – Immingham
IS – Inverness
KD – Carlisle Kingmoor (BR)
LO – Longsight Manchester
ML – Motherwell
NL – Neville Hill Leeds
PO – Privately Owned
SF – Stratford London
SP – Springs Branch Wigan
TE – Thornaby Tees
TI – Tinsley Sheffield
TO – Toton Nottingham
WC – West Coast Railways
YK – York

The driver's assistant on a Class 27 exchanges tokens with the signalman at Crianlarich station. The loco was working the 21.50 London Euston to Fort William sleeper service. This train was worked by an electric loco from London to Mossend, a Class 47 from Mossend Yard to Glasgow Queen Street, and the Class 27 would have been attached from there. (July 1979)

No. 46048 (GD) arrives at the east end of Edinburgh with the 13.20 service from Newcastle. This loco was withdrawn from traffic in September 1981 after sustaining fire damage. (June 1980)

No. 37148 (ED) passes Dalmuir station with a Bowling Oil Terminal to Bishopbriggs tank train. (July 1979)

No. 26036 (HA) arrives at Glasgow Queen Street with ECS from Cowlairs Coaching Depot. This loco was finally broken up at MC Processing, Springburn, in May 1995. (October 1979)

No. 08227 (ED) is seen at Paisley Canal, shunting some mineral wagons for the local coal merchant. The coal yard was to the left of the station. This is the area that was unfortunately sold off by BR in 1986 for houses. The present Paisley Canal station is situated just beyond the brake van. (December 1979)

No. 40150 (HA) arrives at Arbroath with the 09.40 Aberdeen to Glasgow Queen Street service. This loco was withdrawn from traffic in January 1985 and broken up at Doncaster Works by May 1987. (August 1980)

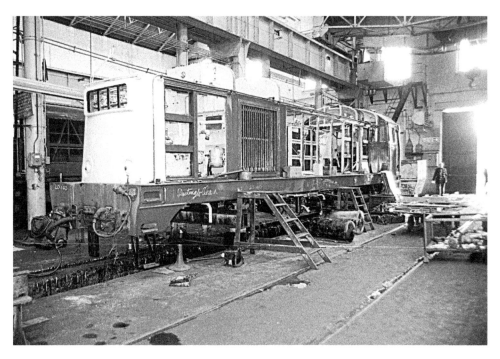

No. 20160 (TO) inside Glasgow Works undergoing a major overhaul. This loco was re-allocated to Bescot Depot from October 1990 but was finally withdrawn from traffic in December 1990. It was finally dismantled at Springburn by May 1994. (August 1980)

No. 25085 (HA) gets the signal at Platform 5 at Aberdeen with the 17.12 service to Montrose. This loco was withdrawn from traffic in March 1982. The semaphore signals were replaced by modern colour light signalling from 1981. (June 1980)

HST No. 254030 (HT) and a Class 47 with various staff meet at Platform 10 at Edinburgh Waverley. (June 1980)

No. 26044 (IS) shunts fertiliser wagons at Forfar Yard. This station was another casualty of Beeching, and the through passenger services between Perth and Aberdeen were withdrawn in 1966. Freight continued on until the summer of 1982. Part of this line between Bridge of Dun and the branch to Brechin still lives on as part of the Caledonian Preserved Railway. (August 1980)

No. 27209 (IS) arrives at Inverurie with the 14.46 Inverness to Aberdeen service. (June 1980)

A Class 40 seen at Platform 10 of Glasgow Central, having arrived with a late-running newspaper service from Manchester Red Bank. (July 1979)

No. 47550 *University of Dundee* (IS) passes the site of Inverkeilor station with the 09.05 Glasgow Queen Street to Inverness via Aberdeen service. This loco was withdrawn from traffic in March 2000. (August 1982)

No. 37120 (TI) at Auchincruive sidings near Ayr. Auchincruive was used by Prestwick Airport to supply aviation fuel and was a back-up to the main supply sidings at Monkton, which are still in use. The last train to use these sidings, however, was in the early 1990s. The track was removed in 2002 and houses have now been built over it. (March 1987)

No. 37403 (ED) at Oban station, having arrived with the 08.20 from Glasgow Queen Street. In my opinion, this was a far superior way to travel than the Class 156 Sprinters, which were introduced from 1988. This loco was withdrawn from traffic in March 2000. It was re-instated shortly afterwards and is still currently in use with DRS, based at Carlisle. (April 1986)

No. 37261 *Caithness* (ML) is seen shunting ballast wagons at Hillhouse Quarry, near Barassie. Ballast trains were regular users of this branch until the quarrying company finished rail contracts in 2001. The Hillhouse spur left the Barassie to Kilmarnock line approximately 1 mile east of Barassie. The track has now been lifted, but strangely one of the semaphore signals within the yard is still on site. (July 1995)

No. 66709 (GB) passes Falkland Yard with a Tyne Yard to Hunterston empty coal train. Note the redundant EWS wagons either side. These were removed shortly after and look likely to be either modified or scrapped. (September 2016)

No. 37137 (ML) and No. 37125 (ML) accelerate away from Kilwinning Junction with a Hunterston to Ravenscraig working. This traffic ceased in May 1992 when Ravenscraig closed. (June 1980)

A Class 37 at Irvine, heading north with a Barony Colliery to Longannet Power Station coal train working. This traffic ceased in 1983. (February 1978)

No. 37170 (HM) at Gretna Junction with a Carlisle to Glasgow Central service via Dumfries and Kilmarnock. Note the WCML to the left of the picture. (May 1983)

No. 47710 (HA) in Princes Street Gardens with a Glasgow Queen Street to Edinburgh service. This loco was finally scrapped at EMR Kingsbury in March 2007. (April 1982)

No. 55016 *Gordon Highlander* (YK) crosses the Tweed on the Royal Border Bridge just south of Berwick station with a Down Saturday relief London King's Cross to Edinburgh service. (July 1981)

No. 47270 (ED) approaches Gatehead level crossing between Kilmarnock and Barassie Junction with a diverted Freightliner service. This service ran from Crewe Basfordhall to Coatbridge FLT and had been diverted off the West Coast Main Line due to engineering work. The train reversed in Barassie Yard before heading north. (November 1988)

The driver of No. 47481 (CD) speaks to the signalman from Platform 3 at Ayr. The driver would probably be confirming that his loco-hauled stock had been coupled up successfully. The loco then worked forward as the 18.45 Ayr to Glasgow Central service. (March 1986)

A Class 47 crosses Ballochmyle Viaduct south of Mauchline with a local service from Carlisle to Glasgow Central. (January 1986)

No. 47108 (ED) at Cummertrees between Dumfries and Annan with the 08.40 Glasgow Central to Carlisle local service. (March 1985)

No. 47270 (HA) passes through Newton station with a football special from Aberdeen to Kings Park. This was for Aberdeen football fans travelling to the match against Glasgow Rangers at Hampden. (May 1982)

A Class 37 passes a Class 20 shunting wagons at Bogside, north of Irvine. Note the snow in the background on the Dalry Hills. The sidings at Bogside were removed in 1984. (February 1978)

A general view of Inverness Depot from a local housing estate. The view shows Class 101 and 120 DMUs, with Mk 1 and 2 coaching stock, which are now all history. (August 1978)

Irvine Yard, from left to right, shows: a Class 26 with a brake van on the main line heading north; a Class 27 in the Down sidings with an engineers' train; and a Class 20 with another brake van waiting to depart. Once again, this shows a type of railway operation that is now in the past. Local trip workings delivering goods for customers were deemed uneconomic and were phased out by the early 1990s. (April 1986)

A Class 37 heading north with a Glasgow Queen Street to Oban service crosses a Class 27 at Ardlui with a southbound engineers' train on the West Highland line. (April 1986)

No. 20005 (HA) passes Dunfermline Townhill Depot with a local trip train from Thornton Yard to Millerhill. Dunfermline Townhill closed in 1987. (April 1983)

No. 47451 (CD) at Brownhill between Dalry and Glengarnock with the 07.55 SX Ayr to Glasgow Central service. This train was loco-hauled at this time due to a shortage of Class 126 DMUs. This shot was taken from high up, from a signal gantry. Note on the left the old track bed of the Kilbarchan Loop lines, which were connected to the main line, coming in from the left. These were removed in 1974. (April 1980)

Driver Ian McGrath of Ardrossan Depot is at the controls of No. 08344 (AY) in Ardrossan Yard. Local trip workings here ceased in May 1984. Most drivers were transferred to Ayr and Corkerhill depots. (May 1982)

No. 40003 (HM) passes the disused station of Drybridge between Kilmarnock and Barassie with the 13.50 Carlisle to Ayr service. (August 1980)

No. 26023 (IS) passes Dundee Central signal box with the 17.12 service from Perth. (August 1981)

No. 47703 *Saint Mungo* (HA) is seen stabled at Haymarket Depot. Going by the oil stains, this loco looks as if something was not quite right with the engine or the fuel supply. (May 1985)

No. 47701 *Saint Andrew* (HA) is seen north of Montrose with the 09.25 Glasgow Queen Street to Aberdeen service. (August 1982)

An HST at Saughton on the outskirts of Edinburgh with a London King's Cross to Aberdeen service. In the background, a Class 26 passes with a coal train, probably bound for Millerhill Yard. (March 1987)

An HST passes New Cumnock with a diverted Glasgow Central to Poole train. This service had been diverted due to engineering work on the WCML. (March 1992)

No. 47009 (GD) at Swinlees, north of Dalry, with a Glasgow Central to Stranraer Harbour service. Note the GUV coach attached on the front and the Class 37s about to pass with a northbound Hunterston to Ravenscraig working. (May 1984)

Millerhill Depot near Edinburgh sees a varied collection of diesel power, which includes Class 26, 37 and 40 locos. (May 1983)

No. 37411 (ED) with an engineers' wagon at Glen Douglas, crossing a northbound passenger working. (April 1986)

No. 44004 (PO) at Springburn Works. This loco was part of the exhibits used during a BR open day. This loco started its life with BR as D4 and was later named *Great Gable*. It was later saved for preservation and is currently based at the Midland Railway Centre at Butterley. (June 1980)

A Class 27/25 combination pass Ben Cruachan power station with an excursion from Edinburgh to Fort William. Ben Cruachan Power Station is a pumped storage hydro power station operated by Scottish Power, which was opened by Her Majesty the Queen in 1965. It can produce electricity for the grid in two minutes – or thirty seconds if its turbines are already primed on 'spinning reserve'. (May 1979)

No. 66553 (FL) at Drybridge between Kilmarnock and Barassie with an empty MGR working from Drax Power Station to Killoch Colliery. Drybridge station was closed in March 1969 when the local service between Kilmarnock and Ayr was withdrawn. (March 2011)

No. 37194 (TI) at Gartcosh Steelworks on the northern side of Glasgow with a steel coil train. The works closed in February 1986. (August 1981)

No. 60060 (TE) near Crawford with the daily oil train working from Dalston near Carlisle to Grangemouth. (November 2001)

No. 25265 (CD) passes Mauchline signal box with a southbound freight from Falkland Yard to Carlisle Kingmoor Yard. (January 1986)

A Class 26 at Georgemas Junction backs onto the Thurso portion of a service from Inverness. This was in the days when trains were split into two portions – one for Thurso and one for Wick. (August 1978)

No. 26012 (HA) passes Lugton signal box with the 08.40 Carlisle to Glasgow Central service. In the background, a Class 20 with a freight working off the Giffen branch near Beith awaits a path back to Mossend Yard with an armaments train. The Giffen branch closed to freight services in 1992 and has only been used for emergency services in 1999 and 2002 to carry out mock accidents. However, the connection to the main line at Lugton was severed in 2009 when the main line was re-doubled between Lugton and Stewarton. Remarkably, most of the single track on the Giffen branch remains in situ, albeit very overgrown. (May 1980)

No. 26014 (ED) and No. 26025 (ED) pass through Auchinleck station with a southbound empty merry-go-round from Falkland Yard to Knockshinnoch Colliery. (March 1987)

Two Class 20s shunt a parcels coach onto the rear of the 08.57 Glasgow Central to Stranraer Harbour service. Parcel coaches or GUVs were a regular feature at this time and were usually removed on arrival at Glasgow Central. They conveyed newspaper traffic and parcels, as well as Red and Night Star parcels. Once again, this is now a thing of the past. (June 1984)

Class No. 20112 (ED) shunts various wagons at High Street Goods Yard, Glasgow. This yard closed in the mid-1980s, but at one time this was one of the busiest rail parcel distribution depots in the UK. (April 1980)

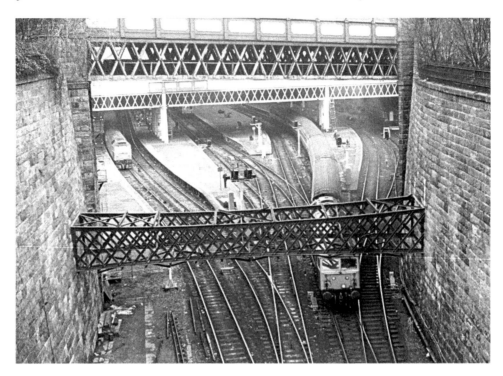

No. 47707 *Holyrood* (HA) departs from Glasgow Queen Street with the 13.30 service to Edinburgh. This view is no longer available due to the building of the Buchanan Street Shopping Centre. (February 1985)

No. 27106 (ED) is seen at Edinburgh Waverley, departing with a local train to Dundee. Note the old North British Hotel in the background. (March 1982)

No. 27004 (ED) departs from Ayr with a parcels train from London Euston to Stranraer Harbour. This loco was withdrawn from traffic in May 1987. Through parcel services ceased around the same time. (May 1986)

No. 40060 (HA) stabled in between duties in the fueling bay at Perth station. This loco was transferred from Haymarket to Carlisle Kingmoor in May 1981. It was withdrawn from traffic in January 1985 and was re-numbered No. 97405 for use during the Crewe station re-modelling. However, it was finally broken up at Vic Berry's scrapyard in Leicester by March 1988. (August 1981)

Nos 20198 and 20189 (both ED) are seen at Ayr Harbour, having just arrived with a loaded MGR from Chalmerston Open Cast Colliery. Ground staff discuss shunting options. (March 1987)

No. 56054 (TE) in the north end of Kilwinning Loop with an engineers' train consisting of La Farge aggregate wagons. This loco was named *British Steel Lllanwhern* at Cardiff in May 1993 without ceremony. (November 1999)

No. 47267 (BR) is at Kilmarnock with a southbound freight from Mossend Yard to Carlisle Yard. The Class 27 was heading north with a freight train and was waiting for the Class 47 to pass to gain access onto the single line to Lugton. Sadly, forty years later this single line still causes congestion with little or no hope of Transport Scotland authorising the reinstatement of double track north of Kilmarnock and between Barrhead and Lugton. (March 1982)

No. 25056 (CD) at Dumfries with the 13.45 Glasgow Central to Carlisle service. Note the old route headcode still displaying the headcode 7F07, though it should have been 1M80. (August 1981)

No. 20089 (ED) is at Larbert with a southbound tank train heading for Mossend Yard. (October 1983)

D5054 or No. 24054 (PO). This loco was allocated to Inverness Depot between January 1961 and October 1966. It is now part of the National Railway Museum collection, based at York. The loco was recorded at the Crewe Heritage Centre. (July 1987)

Above: No. 26036 (IS) at Kyle
of Lochalsh is ready to depart
with a train to Inverness. The
Isle of Skye is in the background.
(August 1981)

Right: No. 47208 (HA), at the
east end of Aberdeen station,
awaits its driver for a service to
Inverness. (August 1981)

Left: A Class 27 shunts oil wagons at Stranraer Harbour. This traffic ceased in the early 1990s. (August 1981)

Below: Nos 37229 and 37029 (both DR) are seen near Catrine with a Pathfinder Railtour, heading from Ayr to Crewe. (July 2007)

No. 26034 (IS) at Thurso station with a service to Inverness. This loco was involved in an accident at Carlisle Kingmoor Yard in August 1989, and was withdrawn from traffic shortly afterwards. It was scrapped at Springburn Works by September 1990.

No. 47816 (CD) is seen near Auchinleck with a diverted Glasgow Central to London Euston service. (March 2004)

The Network Rail HST Measurement train at Edinburgh, also known as the High Speed Banana. This train is seen all over the UK. Note the window box below the windscreen, which houses a high-quality digital camera. (March 2004)

No. 67009 (TO) approaches Inverness with the Safeway container service, heading for Mossend Yard on the outskirts of Glasgow. (June 2004)

No. 66186 (TO) approaches Whifflet with a Mossend to Longannet empty MGR service. (June 2001)

No. 47118 (IS) at sidings adjacent to Inverness station with a southbound Freightliner. (August 1984)

No. 40057 (GD) passes Thornhill signal box north of Dumfries with a return excursion from Ayr to Nelson in Lancashire. (April 1982)

Two Class 37s prepare to depart Hunterston High Level with an MGR service for Ravenscraig No. 2. (May 1983)

No. 37111 (ED) arrives at Edinburgh with the 08.10 SO summer-only service from Glasgow Queen Street to Scarborough. (August 1981)

A Class 47 passes Laurencekirk signal box with the 07.55 Aberdeen to Glasgow Queen Street service. (May 1983)

A GNER HST approaches Haymarket station with the morning Inverness to London King's Cross service. (June 2008)

No. 47427 (ED) is at Montrose with a northbound Freightliner from Portobello, near Edinburgh, to Aberdeen service. This loco was withdrawn from traffic in November 1989 after suffering fire damage and was cut up at MC Processors at Springburn by April 1992. (August 1982)

No. 60090 (TO) approaches Falkland Yard with an Irvine Caledonian Pulp Mill to Burngullow tank service. These tanks were known as the Silver Bullets. They still run once a week. (June 1999)

Inverness Rose Street before colour lights took over. A Class 47 waits to shunt into the nearby depot. (August 1981)

Two Class 31 locos near Mauchline taking the Annbank branch towards Ayr with a Network Rail test train. (April 2010)

No. 66068 (TO) at the Long Lye Sidings in Kilmarnock with a southbound loaded MGR. These sidings were re-laid in 2009 to allow Ayrshire coal workings to reverse, saving valuable time when heading via the coast. These tracks were built over the old track bed of the former Kilmarnock to Dalry line, which was closed in May 1976 and extends approximately 1 mile north of Kilmarnock station towards the village of Knockentiber. This loco was on a Greenburn to Drax working. (April 2010)

No. 47476 (CD) approaches Howwood with the diverted 06.04 Stockport to Glasgow Central service. This was due to engineering work on the WCML, resulting in the service having to be diverted via Kilwinning as there was no path north of Kilmarnock. (April 1993)

No. 26038 (IS) passes through Motherwell with a southbound coal train. (August 1981)

No. 37192 (ED) is seen at Perth with a southbound service to Glasgow Queen Street. (April 1985)

No. 20175 (ED) is seen at Mossend Yard on the rear of an iron ore train with two Class 37s up front. The Class 20 would have been used as a banker up the steep Bellshill Bank due to the weight of the train. (May 1982)

No. 27034 (ED) at Paisley Gilmour Street with the 07.00 Ayr to Glasgow Central service. A Class 303 arrives with a Wemyss Bay to Glasgow Central service in the background. (May 1982)

No. 66097 (TO) emerges from Mossgiel Tunnel, north of Mauchline, and heads north to Kilmarnock Long Lyes with a Greenburn to Drax Power Station loaded MGR. (October 2011)

No. 40165 (HA) is at Cockburnspath with a Glasgow Queen Street to Scarborough service. This loco was withdrawn from traffic shortly after this shot was taken and it was cut up at Doncaster Works by June 1983. (July 1981)

No. 26034 (IS) approaches Thurso with a portion of a service from Inverness. The other portion, which would have gone to Wick, would also be hauled by a Class 26. (August 1981)

No. 57313 (WC) at Kilmarnock en route from Ayr to Carnforth Steam Town with ECS. No. 47760 (WC) was behind the leading loco. (June 2013)

No. 66075 (TI) at Bowhouse, south of Kilmarnock, with an empty MGR from Carlisle Yard to New Cumnock Sidings. The train had run up to Kilmarnock from the Long Lye Sidings and reversed. (October 2013)

No. 47435 (HA) comes off the single line section between Montrose South and Usan with the 14.40 Aberdeen to Edinburgh service. (August 1980)

No. 55020/D9000 (PO) is seen at Stewarton, hauling EMU Class No. 334038 (GW) from Yoker Depot on the north-west side of Glasgow to Brodie Engineering of Kilmarnock for refurbishment. The Deltic was used for most of the period of this contract due to GBRf having a shortage of Class 66 locos. (November 2013)

No. 56105 (CL) is at Barassie with the regular aviation empties, returning from Prestwick Airport to Grangemouth Oil Terminal. (June 2014)

No. 66554 (FL) is at Lochside, north of New Cumnock, with an empty MGR working from Drax Power Station to Killoch Colliery. (June 2014)

No. 47519 (IM) is seen at East Linton with the 09.50 Edinburgh to Sheffield service. There are plans for this station to re-open in the future. (July 1981)

No. 66168 (TO) passes Western Gailes golf course near Barassie with an empty slurry tank train from Irvine Caledonian Pulp Mill to Mossend, near Glasgow. The actual factory is behind the loco. (June 2014)

No. 20111 (HA), at Carstairs, is heading south with an engineers' train from Mossend Yard to Beattock. (August 1981)

No. 60021 (CL) is seen south of New Cumnock with a diverted tank train from Warrington to Larbert. The train had been diverted off the WCML due to a damaged bridge at Lamington caused by Storm Frank. (February 2016)

No. 37426 (ML) is at Stirling with a northbound timber train from Mossend Yard to Millburn Yard, Inverness. (June 2001)

No. 47424 (ED) is at Aviemore with the northbound Clansman, the 09.35 London Euston to Inverness service. (August 1981)

No. 66015 (TO) is seen at near Ochiltree, north of Auchinleck, with a diverted Cartic train from Didcot to Mossend Yard. (February 2016)

No. 66108 (TO) is seen near Tarbolton, between Annbank Junction and Mauchline, with a Pathfinder Railtour working. No. 66092 (TO) is on the rear. The tour ran from Carlisle to Kilmarnock via Kingmoor Yard and visited various branch lines around south-west Scotland. (August 2016)

No. 66711 (GB) is seen at Gailes, between Barassie and Irvine, with an empty MGR from Tyne Yard to Hunterston Clydeport. (September 2016)

No. 40108 (LO) passes Montrose South signal box with an Aberdeen to Mossend freightliner service. (August 1980)

No. 47268 (HA) crosses the Montrose girder bridge south of the station with the 08.40 Edinburgh to Aberdeen service. (August 1981)

No. 47051 (ED) propels ECS into Corkerhill Depot. This train had just arrived at the nearby station on a special from Edinburgh in connection with the papal visit to Glasgow's Bellahouston Park. (June 1982)

No. 40164 (SP) is seen near Paisley Hawkhead with ECS from Corkerhill. The special train had arrived at Corkerhill from Dumfries earlier and the ECS was going to Largs for servicing. This was one of the busiest BR days in Scotland ever. (June 1982)

No. 47410 (GD) is seen at Beattock Summit with a Sunday diverted Glasgow Central to London Euston service. This service was booked via the G&SW but was diverted via the WCML due to engineering work in the Mauchline area. (March 1984)

No. 40022 (SP) is at Usan, near Montrose, with the 13.35 Glasgow Queen Street to Aberdeen service. (August 1980)

No. 40122/D200 (KD) is seen at Kilmarnock with a railtour from Ayr to York organised by the Ayrshire Railway Preservation Group (ARPG). Note the headboard on the front of the loco. (May 1984)

No. 27059 (ED) and driver are seen at Ayr station, awaiting the signal to go forward with a Tyne Yard to Stranraer Town mixed freight. (July 1984)

No. 37021 (ED) is at the buffers at Mallaig station, having just arrived with the 12.55 service from Fort William. (August 1981)

No. 37068 (TE) is seen at Stirling with a Motorail service to London Euston. This loco would work the train as far as Mossend Yard, where an electric loco would take over. (June 1984)

No. 37035 (IS) is seen receiving attention inside Inverness Depot. This loco was withdrawn from traffic in October 1995. It was cut up at Booth Roe Metals of Rotherham by September 1998. (August 1984)

No. 26037 (IS), with failed No. 47307 (TI), approaches Aviemore with the 10.25 Inverness to Edinburgh service. (August 1981)

No. 47593 *Galloway Princess* (ED) arrives at Perth with a Glasgow Queen Street to Aberdeen service. Note the old Midland bus on the road bridge. (May 1984)

No. 47209 (IM) arrives at Perth with the 16.42 Inverness to Edinburgh service. The new relief driver and second man prepare to take over. (August 1981)

No. 27003 (IS) is at Irvine with a southbound freight. This loco was withdrawn from traffic in January 1987 and finally scrapped at MC Metals, Springburn, in December 1987. (December 1982)

No. 47431 (YK) is seen at Dumfries with the 10.15 London Euston to Stranraer Harbour service. Note the collection of trainee drivers about to board the loco with their instructor. (August 1981)

No. 55007 *Pinza* (FP) is spotted at Haymarket Depot. This loco was named at Doncaster Works in June 1961 and was finally cut up at the same location in June 1982. It was named after a famous race horse that won the Derby in 1953. (August 1981)

No. 66177 (TO) is at Ballieston with a Longannet to Hunterston empty MGR service. (May 2014)

Two Class 20s depart Millerhill Yard with a mixed northbound freight. This is approximately the area where the facility for the new ScotRail Class 385 trains is being built. (April 1987)

No. 40164 (SP) is seen passing Corkerhill Depot with a special from Largs to Corkerhill station. (June 1982)

No. 40033 (LO) is seen stabled between duties at Edinburgh Waverley. This loco was named *Empress of England* at Derby Works in September 1961. It was withdrawn from traffic in August 1984 and cut up at Crewe Works by March 1985. (August 1981)

No. 58016 (TO) is at Haymarket Depot. The loco visited the depot as a guest as part of another BR open day. (May 1985)

No. 47547 (CD) is seen at Thornhill with a diverted Glasgow Central to London Euston service. Despite lobbying over the years, this station remains closed, but the old platforms are still in remarkably good condition. (April 1993)

No. 37021 (ED) arrives at Arrochar and Tarbert station with the 07.40 Oban to Glasgow Queen Street service while No. 37114 (ED) heads north to Fort William. Note the GUV parcel coach immediately behind the loco. (August 1981)

Nos 37139 and 37152 (both ML) growl down the line just south of West Kilbride with a Hunterston to Ravenscraig loaded coal train. (August 1983)

A Class 27 crosses the Forth Bridge with a southbound engineers' train. (March 1987)

No. 37212 (ML) is seen at Minnivey station, near Dalmellington, which was the site of the Ayrshire Railway Preservation Group's activities until 2010. The train was a Branch Line Society special from Ayr and was top-and-tailed, with No. 37043 (ML) on the rear. This was the first time that main line locos had reached Minnivey. Chalmerston coal disposal site is situated approximately half a mile behind the train. Scottish Coal operations at Chalmerston ceased around 2008 and do not look likely to resume. (August 1996)

No. 47703 *Saint Mungo* (HA) is seen at Aberdeen with a southbound push-pull service to Glasgow Queen Street. (January 1987)

Two Class 37s are seen near Hollybush, on the Chalmerston branch, with a loaded MGR from Chalmerston to Ayr Harbour service. (May 1998)

No. 31323 (IM) approaches Drem with a special from York to Edinburgh. This loco was withdrawn from traffic in June 1989 after sustaining fire damage and was eventually cut up at MC Processors, Springburn, by September 1991. (August 1981)

No. 47552 (BR) approaches Greenock Central with ECS from Polmadie CSD to form an advertised day excursion from Gourock to Sunderland. (April 1989)

No. 56079 (ML) is on the Killoch branch near Mossblown with a loaded MGR from Chalmerston to Killoch Colliery. This coal would be sweetened at Killoch before being taken back to Ayr Harbour for shipment to Northern Ireland. (August 1994)

No. 47615 *Caerphilly Castle/Castell Caerffili* (SP) approaches Ayr with the midday Paddy boat train service from Stranraer Harbour to Glasgow Central. This loco was re-numbered to 47747 in February 1994 and was put into storage at Crewe Diesel Depot in October 2002. However, it met its end at Booths of Rotherham, being cut up by June 2013. (March 1986)

No. 37025 (IS) is seen at Inverness TMD. This loco was eventually withdrawn from traffic in February 1999 and was later sold to the SRPS at Bo'ness in August 2000. (August 1984)

No. 37428 (ML) is seen at Ayr station with the Royal Scotsman luxury railtour train. This train visits various scenic locations in Scotland, mainly on the west coast, and is generally frequented by wealthy Americans. On this day the train was being prepared for a departure to Bridge of Orchy. (April 1998)

A Class 27 approaches Haymarket station with the 06.21 Dundee to Edinburgh local service. (March 1983)

No. 40027 *Parthia* (LO) is seen at Kilmarnock with the 07.15 Nottingham to Glasgow Central service. This was the last remnant of the old Thames–Clyde Express. Note the steam heating escaping from most of the coaches. It was a bitterly cold Christmas Eve. (December 1981)

A triple-headed Class 56 is seen working at Falkland Yard, hooking up to wagons for the south. This train consisted of No. 56126 (IM) hauling failed No. 56104 (IM) and additional failure No. 56131 (IM). The two rearmost failures were presumably being taken back to their home depot for attention. (July 1998)

No. 60076 (TO) approaches Holehouse Junction on the Chalmerston branch with a Falkland Yard to Broomhill Open Cast Mine working. The loco had a brake van at the rear and would be propelled onto the Broomhill branch after the shunter had operated a ground frame. This open cast site was short lived, only being open from 1998 until 2001. (September 1998)

A Class 47 passes Auldgirth signal box with a Carlisle to Glasgow Central service. On this day the train was running approximately thirty minutes late due to suspected defective coaches being removed. This signal box was closed a year later. (April 1982)

No. 47420 (FP) is at Leuchars station with the 14.05 Birmingham New Street to Aberdeen service. (August 1981)

Nos 26005 and 26026 (both ED) are seen hauling a failed HST at New Cumnock on the 10.25 Edinburgh to Poole service. The train was running nearly three hours late due to the HST failing at Barrhead. (August 1992)

No. 37051 (ML) arrives with a failed Class 47 in tow at Platform 3 at Glasgow Central with the 11.10 Carlisle to Glasgow Central service. (September 1986)

No. 26034 (IS) shunts a mineral wagon at Thurso Yard. This loco was finally scrapped by September 1990 at MC Processing, Springburn. (August 1981)

No. 20002 (ED) is seen at Fort William station, carrying out shunting duties. This loco was withdrawn from service in February 1988 and was cut up at MC Processors in Springburn, Glasgow, by May 1990. (August 1981)

No. 37694 *Lass of Ballochmyle* (ED) and No. 37194 (ED) both arrive at Ayr Harbour with a loaded MGR from Knockshinnoch. This coal would then be loaded onto a boat for Kilroot Power Station in Northern Ireland. (October 1990)

Nos 20212 and 20211 (both ED) approach Byrehill Junction, south of Kilwinning, with a special Branch Line Train, which had started at Crewe. (May 1984)

No. 70006 (FL) is seen at Falkland Yard with a Drax to Hunterston empty MGR service. (May 2011)

No. 37427 (ML) is seen at Drem with a Binliner train service from Powderhall to Oxwellmains. This flow finished at the end of 2016. This loco was withdrawn from traffic in October 2012 and was cut up at Booths of Rotherham by February 2013. (June 2004)

No. 47704 *Dunedin* (HA) approaches Haymarket with the 11.30 Glasgow Queen Street to Edinburgh service. (August 1981)

No. 33116 *Hertfodshire Railtours* and No. 33109 *Captain Bill Smith RNR* (both SL) pass New Cumnock, hauling SUB stock coaches back to Eastleigh. This special was returning back south after assisting in filming for the movie *Mission Impossible*, starring Tom Cruise. (May 1995)

No. 46029 (GD) arrives at Edinburgh with an excursion service from Ipswich. This loco was withdrawn from traffic in January 1983 and was finally cut up at Swindon Works by September 1986. (August 1981)

No. 66155 (TO) approaches Annbank Junction with a loaded MGR from Falkland Yard to Ratcliffe Power Station. (June 2005)

No. 45043 *The Kings Own Royal Border Regiment* (TO) approaches Byrehill Junction, south of Kilwinning, with the 07.07 Stevenston to Haverton Hill anhydrous ammonia tank train. ICI Stevenston closed its doors in 1987. (April 1982)

No. 40057 (GD) approaches Irvine with an advertised day return excursion from Largs to Manchester Victoria. (April 1982)

No. 66524 (FL) approaches Carstairs with an empty MGR from Drax Power Station to Hunterston Clyde Port. Most of the coal workings from the English power stations ran via the G&SW, but some also run via the ECML and WCML as required. (March 2013)

No. 47456 (CD) is seen at Auldgirth with the 11.00 Stranraer Harbour to London Euston service. These loco-hauled services were replaced by Class 156 Sprinters from October 1988. (October 1984)

No. 60064 (TO) approaches Knockshinnoch Open Cast Colliery with an empty MGR from Ayr Harbour. (May 1997)

No. 26031 (IS) is seen with her driver at Thurso station, having just arrived with the morning service from Inverness. This loco was withdrawn from traffic in April 1989 due to fire damage and was finally cut up at MC Metals at Springburn by September 1990. (August 1981)

No. 66076 (TO) is near Ochiltree with a loaded southbound MGR working from Killoch to Drax. (September 2012)

No. 47416 (CD) arrives at Perth with an Aberdeen to Glasgow Queen Street service. (August 1981)

No. 47001 (HA) is seen at Millerhill Yard, having arrived with a mixed freight from Mossend Yard. This loco was withdrawn from traffic in November 1986 and was finally cut up at Booths of Rotherham by January 1994. (July 1982)

No. 47102 (ED) arrives at Perth with the 09.39 Dundee to Glasgow Queen Street service. (August 1981)

Two Class 67s are seen at Platform 11, Glasgow Central, having arrived with the overnight sleeper from London Euston. No. 67016 (TO) was leading. This service had been diverted via the G&SW due to engineering work on the WCML. (March 2004)

The view from a Mk 1 carriage being hauled by a Class 37 on a Glasgow Queen Street to Oban service, which at this point was approaching Craigendoran Junction, south of Helensburgh. This is where the North Electric lines splits with the West Highland lines. (August 1983)

Above: No. 60033 *Anthony Ashley Cooper* (TO) is seen at Blackhouse Junction, east of Ayr, with a Hunterston to Drax Power Station gypsum special. (August 2001)

Below left: No. 60082 *Mam Tor* (TO) is seen at Heathfield, east of Ayr, on the line to Annbank Junction with an empty MGR from Falkland Yard to Knockshinnoch Open Cast Coal Point working. (July 1998)

Below right: Nos 37071 and 37080 (both ML) are seen at Blackhouse Junction, near Ayr, with a loaded MGR from Falkland Yard to Killoch working. (July 1994)

No. 37520 (ML) is seen near Auchinleck with a diverted Virgin service to London Euston from Glasgow Central. Note the driving van trailer (DVT) immediately behind the loco. A Class 87 was also on the rear. This loco was withdrawn from traffic in February 2007 and was disposed of at TJ Thomson at Stockton by October 2007. (March 1998)

Two Class 20s are seen at Blackfaulds Cutting, near Cumnock, with a Hunterston to Sellafield, Cumbria, nuclear flask service. (February 2001)

No. 59204 (HQ) is seen at Annbank Junction with a loaded MGR test run from Killoch Colliery to Falkland Yard. The test was successful and heralded the onslaught of the Class 66s to the area from 1998. (May 1995)

Right: Two Class 37s approach Rutherglen Old station with a Hunterston to Ravenscraig iron ore working. (September 1980)

Below left: No. 27052 (HA) is seen on the pits inside Haymarket Depot. This depot became a Sprinter-only depot from 1988. This loco was withdrawn from traffic in July 1987; it was finally cut up at Vic Berry's scrapard in Leicester by September 1987. (August 1985)

Below right: No. 26008 (HA) approaches Stranraer Harbour with 3S07, the 09.30 parcels service from London Euston. (April 1983)

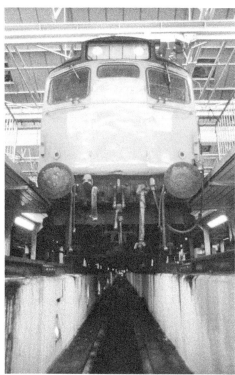

No. 47077 *North Star* (CF) is at Dundee with the 19.25 sleeper service from Aberdeen to London King's Cross. (August 1981)

No. 47408 (GD) is seen near Inverkeilor with the 09.25 Aberdeen to Glasgow Queen Street service. (August 1982)

No. 56035 (TO) is at St Quivox, near Mossblown, east of Ayr, on the Mauchline to Ayr line with a loaded MGR from Killoch Colliery to Ayr Harbour working. (September 2000)